TRI-JETS

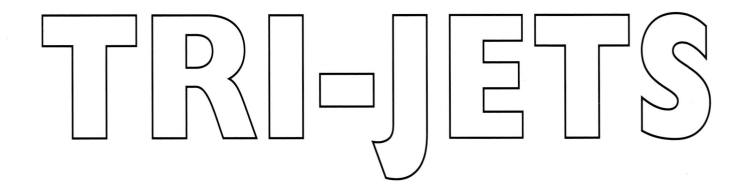

TRI-JETS

ROBBIE SHAW

OSPREY
AEROSPACE

First published in Great Britain in 1996
by Osprey, an imprint of Reed Consumer
Books Limited, Michelin House,
81 Fulham Road, London SW3 6RB and
Auckland, Melbourne, Singapore and Toronto.

ISBN 1 85532 592 6

Editor Tony Holmes
Page design Paul Kime
Printed in Hong Kong

Title page DC-10 or MD-11? The lineage is obvious, and with outer wings and winglets not visible it is virtually impossible to distinguish between the two McDonnell Douglas tri-jets, particularly as American Airlines operates both types. The aircraft in this photograph, taken at Heathrow on 8 February 1994, is in fact an MD-11

Right A Premiair DC-10-10 about to land at Las Palmas. The lack of the fuselage mounted centre bogie which was incorporated on later models is evident in this rear view

For a catalogue of all books published by Osprey Automotive
please write to:

**The Marketing Department, Reed Consumer Books,
1st Floor, Michelin House, 81 Fulham Road, London SW3 6RB**

Introduction

In the space of two-and-a-half months in the autumn of 1970, the world's first two wide-bodied tri-jets took to the air on their maiden flights. Throughout the next decade these two aircraft, the McDonnell Douglas DC-10 and the Lockheed L-1011 TriStar, fought for supremacy in the battle for orders – a battle which initially swung like a pendulum, with Lockheed taking an early lead. However, in the end it was the DC-10 which was declared the winner, with a total production run of 446 aircraft, set against the 250 amassed by its rival. The DC-10 production run also lasted six years longer.

Both types were conceived through an American Airlines requirement for a twin-jet capable of transcontinental range. Ultimately, however, both manufacturers opted for a tri-jet layout, as the engines then available failed to give a 'twin' the performance specified by American. Furthermore, Lockheed had experienced severe pressure from prospective customers Eastern and TWA in favour of a three-engined layout – both operators ultimately selected the L-1011 in serious quantities.

As for Douglas, their design proposal was physically larger than that originally specified by American, so a tri-jet was the only way forward. Fortunately, their prospective launch customer was eventually convinced of this as well, and American signed on the dotted line with an order for 25 aircraft.

The late 1960s and early 70s was perhaps the last great boon period enjoyed by the US civil aviation industry, with the Douglas and Lockheed products having taken to the skies just a year after Boeing's prototype 747. Although possessing a 'wide-body'

layout like the 'Jumbo', the TriStar and DC-10 began to find their own niché market with airlines who could either not afford to buy a 747, or could not justify such a high-capacity aircraft on thinner routes.

Over the years both manufacturers attempted to serve this unique market by offering a variety of versions of their products, and very quickly their efforts were rewarded with export orders. The tri-jets' impressive performance figures also allowed airlines to enjoy 'wide-bodied' load factors at airports which could not take the larger and heavier 747.

Later in their respective production careers, both types 'joined up' for military service in the tanker/cargo/passenger role. In the case of the DC-10, 60 newly-built aircraft were phased into USAF service in the 1980s as KC-10 Extenders, whilst more recently a pair of ex-Martinair DC-10s have been converted into KDC-10 configuration for the Royal Netherlands Air Force. In the case of the TriStar, nine former British Airways aircraft were converted for use by the RAF in the 1980s.

As examples of the DC-10 and L-1011 enter the twilight of their respective careers with 'premier' operators the world over, they are being replaced with more efficient, and youthful, equipment. However, many tri-jets are entering further employment amongst Third World airlines, charter operators and freight carriers, the latter finding the 'wide-body' design ideal for their purposes.

Building on the success of its DC-10, McDonnell Douglas opted for a lookalike successor in the MD-11. Being slightly longer than its predecessor, and featuring winglets for improved aerodynamic per-

Above *Former Hawaiian TriStar 50 N763BE now serves with Rich International, in whose service it wears a rather uninspiring grey and white livery. The aircraft is seen about to touchdown at Gatwick at the end of a transatlantic charter flight*

formance, the MD-11 looked a very promising prospect indeed, and initial orders confirmed this. Unfortunately for McDonnell Douglas it soon became apparent that the MD-11 was not meeting its range/payload specs, and there was much grumbling among customer airlines – Garuda Indonesia even threatened to refuse to take delivery of its first aircraft until these problems were solved. The manufacturer has rectified a number of the shortfalls at no cost to the customer, but the damage has been done.

Airline confidence in this sleek-looking tri-jet is obviously low, and one operator has announced that it is to convert all five of its aircraft into freighters

after less than five years of service. Indeed, the largest operator of the type, American Airlines, is to sell off the bulk of its MD-11s to Federal Express, who will also convert them into freighters. If it can overcome the concerns over its performance then the MD-11 will undoubtedly be a success, but the damage already inflicted may prove fatal for McDonnell Douglas.

At the time of writing there are no other 'widebodied' tri-jets either in production or planned.

All photographs were taken by the author on Kodachrome 64 film, using Nikon F801S cameras and associated lenses. Finally, I would like to thank my wife Eileen for once again providing her unstinting support for my latest project, and giving my raw prose a thorough proof-reading.

Robbie Shaw
December 1995

Contents

Right *Three of Caledonian's TriStars rest at Gatwick between flights on 6 April 1994, whilst a DC-10 can be seen lurking further down the ramp*

DC-10

The DC-10 was conceived in 1966 through a request from American Airlines to seven manufacturers, the operator stating its requirement for a *twin*-jet 'mini-jumbo' primarily for use on non-stop transcontinental services. The Douglas Aircraft Company responded with a proposal for a *tri*-jet, dubbed the DC-10. Although slightly larger than the specification issued by American, and possessing an extra engine which

added to the cost of operating the new jet, the airline succumbed and placed an order for 25 aircraft, with options on a further 25.

The maiden flight of the prototype took place at Douglas's Long Beach facility on 29 August 1970, by which time it had become a division of the giant McDonnell Douglas Corporation.

The initial variant was the DC-10-10 series

powered by General Electric CF6-6D, or -6D1, engines producing 40,000 and 41,000 lbs of thrust respectively. Passenger capacity could be varied from 270 in a mixed configuration, up to 380 in an all-economy fit – the fuselage cross-section is wide enough to permit nine-abreast seating in a two/five/two split in economy, which can be reduced to six-abreast two/two/two in first class.

From the outset, McDonnell Douglas had envisaged several variants of the DC-10, including a long range version for intercontinental routes. This was initially known as the DC-10-20, and was developed in response to a request from Northwest Orient. On this variant the wingspan was increased by three metres (9 ft 10 in), and fuel capacity by an amazing two-thirds. To cope with the extra weight, a

Above *American Airlines recently placed its older DC-10-10s in desert storage, but many remain in use on domestic services including flights to Honolulu, where N118AA is seen coming into land*

Left *American Airlines DC-10-30 N137AA thunders out of Gatwick. The airline's DC-10s are no longer used on international services, having been replaced by more fuel-efficient Boeing 767s and MD-11s*

Above *American Airlines DC-10-30 lines up prior to departing from runway 08R at Gatwick, bound for Dallas/Fort Worth. This route is now shared by the airline's Boeing 767 and MD-11 fleet*

Left *Older variants of both the DC-10 and L-1011 are still used extensively on US domestic routes. Heading the queue at the holding point at Los Angeles is an American Airlines DC-10-10, followed by a Delta Airlines L-1011-1*

third main undercarriage bogie was installed in the fuselage. The Northwest machines were powered by Pratt & Whitney JT9D-20 turbofans rated at 49,000 lbs with water-injection. The first series -20 aircraft flew on 28 February 1972. Northwest was the only customer for the DC-10-20, and the variant was later redesignated as the DC-10-40.

In June 1972 the first DC-10-30 flew, and featured the increased wing span, fuel capacity and undercarriage bogie of the -20. This variant was powered by General Electric turbofans producing up to 51,000 lbs of thrust. It also became the most prolific of all variants, its intercontinental range of 9544 km (5150 nm) compared to 6768 km (3652 nm) on the series -10 being a major factor in its export success

The DC-10-40 powered by JTD-59A engines rated at 53,000 lbs thrust first flew on 25 July 1975, with Japan Air Lines being the only customer – the Northwest machines so redesignated are not true -40s. The next variant from the Long Beach production line was the -30ER, this

suffix standing for extended range. An additional 5807-litre fuel tank was installed in the rear cargo compartment on this model, increasing its range by up to 370 km (200 nm), whilst a larger 12,556-litre tank was also made available. Swissair ordered the first two -30ER variants in 1980, as well as kits to convert a further two aircraft already in service. The first large tank to be installed was on a Finnair aircraft, enabling the airline to operate a direct flight over the North Pole from Helsinki to Tokyo, a distance of 11,056 km (5966 nm). To cope with the weight of the additional fuel, more powerful CF6-50C2B engines producing 54,000 lbs of thrust was used on the -30ER.

Produced in fewer numbers than any other variant was the DC-10-15, which was designed specifically to meet the requirements of Aeromexico and Mexicana for hot and high operations. This aircraft is basically a series -10 airframe with the powerful engines used on the -30, hence the out of sequence designation. The match of airframe and engines enables both operators to carry maximum payloads out of Mexico City, which is situated some 7000 ft above sea level. The first flight of this variant took

Above Wearing Continental Airlines' old colour scheme, DC-10-30 N13067 is seen about to touchdown at Gatwick. This aircraft began its career with Alitalia in 1974 as I-DYNB, before being sold to Eastern Airlines in 1985. In September 1990 it was delivered to Continenta,l with whom it is still in daily use

Right Continental's DC-10-30 N14063 is captured on final approach to Gatwick. Affiliate Continental Micronesia uses six short-range DC-10-10s from Guam on Polynesian routes

place on 8 January 1981, with deliveries to Mexicana commencing in June. The Mexican airlines were the only customers for the series -15, with just seven aircraft being built!

In addition to the passenger variants described above, McDonnell Douglas also produced two dedicated freighter models, the first being the DC-10-30CF. This is a convertible freighter which can be used in either all-cargo or all-passenger configurations, or a combination of both. The first CF was a series -30 aircraft which first flew on 28 February 1973, and initial deliveries went to Overseas National and Trans International. The CF was, however, available in any basic series, and Continental bought a number of -10CF aircraft. The final type to be developed was the pure freighter DC-10F, which like the -CF can carry palletised loads. The first of nine aircraft for Federal Express was delivered on 24 January 1986.

Although not featured in this volume, mention should be made of the KC-10A Extender. This is the designation given to the DC-10 variant produced for the United States Air Force in response to a requirement for an advanced tanker/cargo aircraft. On 19 December 1977 it was announced that the McDonnell Douglas product had been selected in preference to the Boeing 747. The KC-10A is based on the airframe of the DC-10-30CF, but has additional modifications for its military role including a 'flying boom' and a hose-drum unit for the in-flight refuelling task, as well as a refuelling receptacle just above the cockpit to enable the Extender to take on fuel itself. The aircraft also has additional fuel cells in

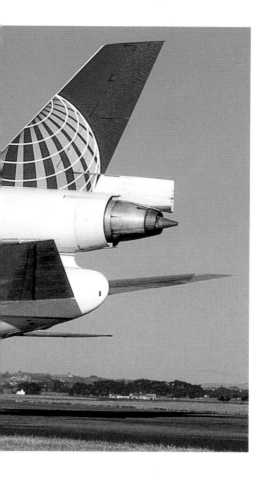

the lower fuselage. The USAF took delivery of 60 KC-10A aircraft, all but one of which are still in use.

After a production run of nearly 20 years, the 446th, and final, DC-10 was delivered to Nigeria Airways in February 1989, this production figure including the USAF's 60 KC-10As. As these words are written, some 350 of the type are still in use worldwide, although many of the older series -10 aircraft have now been placed in desert storage. The series -30 aircraft are in high demand on the second-hand market, however, and two Russian operators, Avcom and Kras Air, have recently taken delivery of the type. British charter airlines Excalibur and Monarch have also just announced that they are to acquire the type for use on intercontinental routes, while freight airline DAS Air Cargo is about to take delivery of its first machine as they start to replace their ageing fleet of noisy Boeing 707s.

Despite its age there is plenty of life yet in the DC-10, and it is not inconceivable that the aircraft will still be in use 25 years from now – the environmentalist and noise lobbies permitting.

Above left *Continental's once bright distinctive livery is now but a faded memory amongst airline enthusiasts the world over, having been replaced by this rather insipid 'corporate white' livery in 1992. N68065 is one of 14 DC-10-30s presently in use, and was photographed at Auckland, New Zealand – a destination no longer served by Continental. The airline has recently disposed of all but two of its ageing Boeing 747s, whilst the delivery of the first 767 has been postponed for at least a year due to fiscal hardships*

Left *Like Continental, Northwest Airlines still uses a sizeable fleet of DC-10s, whose number was enhanced in 1991 with the acquisition of eight former Swissair series -30 machines. With the Kilpatrick Hills in the background, DC-10-40 N148US lines up on runway 23 at Glasgow/Abbotsinch, bound for Boston, a route which was discontinued in 1994*

Above left A Northwest Airlines DC-10-40 comes in 'over the fence' at Detroit Metropolitan airport. The fuselage-mounted centre-line bogie is clearly visible in this view

Left Northwest's current livery is portrayed in evening light conditions as N133JC approaches Detroit Metropolitan. This aircraft is a series -40, and was delivered to Northwest in 1972 as N143US. It was then sold to Jet Charter Service, and is currently leased from Investors Asset Holding Corporation. Northwest operates 29 DC-10s, which supplement Boeing 747s on its international routes

Above Amid great secrecy in February 1993, United unveiled its new livery, which many have since commented is not unlike that of British Airways and Canadian Airlines International. With its DC-10s now appearing in the latest livery, the airline obviously intends to continue operating its tri-jets for some time yet. Aircraft N1844U is a series -10 machine, and was photographed on approach to Los Angeles in March 1995

Overleaf Another American carrier still operating an extensive DC-10 fleet is United Airlines. It has 38 series -10 and -30 DC-10 aircraft which have been used primarily on domestic services since the introduction of the airline's Boeing 747-400s. DC-10-30CF was snapped in the company's old colour scheme during a visit to Auckland in February 1993. This route is now served by a 747-400

Right *The name Western Airlines disappeared on 1 April 1987 when the company was taken over by Delta Airlines. Seen here landing at Honolulu in Western's livery is DC-10-10 N914WA, which was operated by Delta for 18 months before being sold to Scanair. It currently serves with Premiair*

Below right *Leisure Air was a US charter operator which, until its demise early in 1995, operated a fleet of A320s and DC-l0s. In this photograph DC-10-30 N832LA is seen on the runway at Stansted on 12 July 1994, following the completion of the inaugural flight of a new weekly San Francisco service*

Below *Sun Country Airlines is a US charter airline operating a fleet of Boeing 727s and DC-10s. Its aircraft are frequently seen at Las Vegas, although DC-10-10 N572SC was photographed arriving at Detroit Metropolitan inbound from the gambling mecca*

Left Federal Express was a late recipient of the DC-10, acquiring a number of the final batch built. These series -30F freighters are in use on the company's extensive worldwide network, and despite the delivery of MD-11s, the parcel delivery giant has still found time to add to its DC-10 inventory from a variety of sources. Although the company title has now changed to Fedex – a name used unofficially for many years – it will be some time before its large fleet of aircraft wear the new company 'uniform'. Seen in its old livery. DC-10-30F N309FE banks onto the final approach path for runway 13 at Kai Tak

Below left Although devoid of titles, there is no mistaking Canadian Pacific's distinctive orange livery. When this photograph was taken in the summer of 1987 the airline was in the process of amalgamating with Pacific Western, the result of which was the formation of Canadian Airlines International. DC-10-30ER C-GCPE, seen here at Kai Tak, was to become the first of the type to be painted in the new livery

Right *C-GCPG was also repainted in Canadian Airlines International's new BA-style livery, and is seen here at Kai Tak taxying out at the start of a transpacific flight to North America*

Left *Viasa of Venezuela took delivery of its first DC-10 in 1978, with the type being immediately put to use replacing DC-8s on intercontinental routes. The airline operates five series -30 aircraft, including YV-136C photographed rotating from Heathrow's runway 27L*

Above Despite the acquisition of MD-11s, Varig has given no indication that it is going to retire its nine-strong DC-10 fleet. Indeed, as the Brazilian flag carrier is in the process of disposing of all of its 747s in order to bring operating costs down, the DC-10s are likely to be more heavily utilised. Basking in the tropical sun at Rio de Janeiro's Galeao International airport is DC-10-30 PP-VMA, the first of its type to be delivered to the airline back in May 1974

Left Viasa's orange tail markings stand out well against the clear blue skies as DC-10-30 YV-135C climbs away from Amsterdam Schiphol airport. Note how the centre-line bogie retracts forwards whilst the main bogies retract sideways into the belly

Right *Uruguayan airline Pluna has expanded its capacity considerably by leasing Varig's DC-10-30 PP-VMW. This photograph was taken in October 1994, and shows the jet at Rio de Janeiro during the outbound leg of a regular service from Montevideo*

Below right *Now amalgamated into Air France, UTA (Union de Transports Aeriens) was once France's largest independent airline, with an extensive intercontinental network which extended through Africa, Polynesia and as far as New Zealand. Photographed at Auckland is DC-10-30 F-BTDD, an aircraft now in service with yet another French carrier, AOM Airlines*

Below *A long-established DC-10 operator, Swissair was also an early customer for its replacement, the MD-11. Taxying onto the Geneva ramp is DC-10-30ER HB-IHM, photographed in April 1991 – just after the airline had taken delivery if its first two MD-11s*

Right *Looking factory-fresh in the Geneva sunshine is Swissair's DC-10-30ER HB-IHM*

Above A subsidiary of SAS, Stockholm-based charter airline Scanair started operations with a fleet of MD-80s and DC-10s, the latter comprising four DC-10-10s. SE-DHU is seen under tow at its home base

Left During the winter of 1993/94 Scanair amalgamated with Conair of Denmark, the new company being known as Premiair. Its fleet comprises A320s and DC-10s, painted up in a simple all-white scheme, with orange and blue circles representing the sun and sea on the fin of their aircraft. Premiair's fleet is heavily utilised, conveying Scandinavian tourists to Europe's holiday hot-spots, including many flights to the Canary Islands and Las Palmas in particular. Illustrated is DC-10-10 SE-DHU, which was featured earlier in this chapter as N914WA of Western Airlines

Above One of Frankfurt's distinctive lime green tugs pushes back Lufthansa DC-10-30 D-ADGO. This aircraft was delivered to the airline in January 1975, but like the rest of the tri-jet fleet, has since been disposed of. Note other DC-10s of Lufthansa and Condor in the background

Left A Lufthansa DC-10-30 is replenished between flights at Frankfurt

Above *Condor Flugdienst is a subsidiary of Lufthansa, and operates a large inclusive tour charter network to destinations throughout Europe, North America, the Caribbean and the Far East. The fleet is dominated by a sizeable fleet of Boeing 757s and 767s, supplemented by five DC-10-30s. In this shot D-ADSO is seen seconds away from landing at Las Palmas, in the Canary Islands*

Right *With the sun glinting off its prominent canary yellow tail, Condor DC-10-30 D-ADSO awaits its turn to depart Las Palmas*

Above *Formed in 1994, Challengair is a Belgian charter operator which uses a single DC-10-30, registered OO-JOT*

Above left *The first airline to put the MD-11 into service was Finnair, who selected the new McDonnell Douglas tri-jet to replace its fleet of four DC-10s. Although four MD-11s have now been delivered to the Finnish flag carrier, the airline has not ended its association with the earlier tri-jet, however, as one is still in use and other three have been leased out. DC-10-30 OH-LHB was photographed on a rare visit to London/Heathrow*

Left *Iberia received its first DC-10 (EC-CBN) in 1973, and it became the first DC-10 to be lost when it crashed in December of that year while on approach to Boston, fortunately without loss of life. The Spanish airline still uses seven DC-10s to supplement its Boeing 747s on intercontinental routes, and in this view DC-10-30 EC-CEZ* Costa del Azahar *is seen about to touchdown on runway 31R at New York's John F. Kennedy International Airport*

Above As Alitalia disposed of its DC-10s some time ago, the appearance in June 1994 of DC-10-30 N68080 in the Italian flag carrier's colours came as something of a pleasant surprise to European airliner enthusiasts. All was revealed, however, when the port side of the aircraft was viewed, as it was painted up in Continental Airlines' colours. The reason for this DC-10 having a 'split personality' is that a joint marketing agreement had been initiated between the two airlines to publicise their New York/Newark - Rome service

Right Although a TriStar operator since the 1970s, British Airways (BA) also 'got into' DC-10s when it inherited eight series -30s aircraft following its take-over of British Caledonian in 1988. It has been reported that the airline initially did not want the DC-10s, but has since been very pleased indeed with the McDonnell-Douglas product. The type is still in use predominantly on US routes from BA's London/Gatwick base

Left *British Airways has christened its DC-10s after British forests, with the name* New Forest *being applied to G-MULL. Initially delivered to Ariana Afghan Airlines in September 1979, this aircraft was bought by British Caledonian in 1985*

Below *There really couldn't be a more appropriately-registered aircraft than G-DCIO. In 1981 this DC-10-30 was delivered new to British Caledonian, with whom it was named* Flora McDonald. *Acquired by British Airways in the April 1988 takeover, it now flies as* Epping Forest

Left *Looking immaculate in the January sunshine G-NIUK* Cairn Edward Forest *sets off on yet another transatlantic journey. This aircraft began its career in June 1974 as Air Zaire's 9Q-CLT, before being bought by British Caledonian in June 1985. In the spring of 1995, just a few months after this photograph was taken, British Airways leased the aircraft to its then subsidiary, Caledonian Airways. Initially British Airways intended to dispose of the DC-10s once its Boeing 777s were delivered, but it now appears there are no immediate plans to sell-off the tri-jets. Indeed, one of the two on lease to Caledonian returned to the flag carrier at the end of 1995*

Below left *Climbing out of Gatwick bound for Atlanta as flight BA227 is DC-10-30 G-BEBM* Sherwood Forest. *This aircraft was initially ordered by China Airlines, but they pulled out of the contract before it was delivered. It was subsequently delivered to British Caledonian in February 1977 and christened* Robert Burns – The Scottish Bard

Inset *British Caledonian DC-10-30 G-BEBM* Robert Burns – The Scottish Bard *taxies to its parking spot at Gatwick's Pier 2. When in BCAL service the DC-10s flew not just to North America, but also to Africa and Hong Kong*

Right *To supplement its Lockheed TriStars Caledonian Airways leased a DC-10-30 from British Airways in the spring of 1993. The airline names its aircraft after Scottish lochs, with G-BHDH carrying the title* Loch Torridon

Left Displaying Caledonian's golden lion rampant, this DC-10 is seen climbing out of Gatwick. Although Caledonian is a charter airline, its two DC-10s also undertake some scheduled services to the Caribbean for British Airways. Early in 1995 the flag carrier sold its shares in Caledonian to the Inspirations holiday group

Below left Wearing the distinctive colours of Novair International Airways, DC-10-10 G-BJZE is seen about to land at its Gatwick base. This aircraft was one of three operated by the charter airline until it ceased operations in 1990 – it was previously known as Cal-Air, a charter subsidiary of British Caledonian Airways. This particular aircraft was delivered to Laker Airways in March 1979 as G-GSKY Californian Belle

Below Skyjet is a Brussels-based charter operator of a single DC-10-30 which spends most of its time sub-leased to other European carriers. More recently it has formed a subsidiary, Skyjet Brazil, based in Sao Paulo using a former Lufthansa DC-10. The aircraft featured here, V2-LEA, has had an illustrious career, being delivered to KLM as PH-DTE as long ago as February 1973. It subsequently saw service with both SAS and JAT - Yugoslav Airlines

Above *Photographed inbound to London/Heathrow is Zambia Airways DC-10-30 N3016Z Nkwazi. This aircraft served as the airline's flagship from its delivery in July 1984 until the Zambian flag carrier ceased operations in the early summer of 1995. N3016Z is now in service with Monarch Airlines*

Above right *Nigeria Airways is another African state carrier believed to be in financial difficulties. Most of the aircraft in the fleet, including Boeing 737s and Airbus A310s, allegedly remain unairworthy. Nigeria Airways were the recipient of the last DC-10 built, although this aircraft (5N-ANN) was delivered as long ago as 1976*

Right *During 1995 the DC-10 has made an appearance in Russian skies with no less than three different operators: Avcom uses one aircraft for ad-hoc freight work, although the aircraft seems to spend most of its time sitting on the ground at Amsterdam/Schiphol; Aeroflot - Russian International Airlines has just taken delivery of the first of two it intends to use on international freight services; and privately-owned Kras Air took delivery of the first of two DC-10-30s it has on order. The latter operator's first aircraft (N525MD) was photographed at Phoenix/Sky Harbor airport in March 1995*

Left Without doubt one of the most attractive liveries around is that of Ghana Airways, and it is frequently seen in European skies as DC-10-30 9G-ANA is a regular visitor to Dusseldorf and London/Heathrow. In 1994 the airline acquired an MD-11 on lease from World Airways for use on its new Accra - New York route

Below left Ghana Airways' livery comprises the colours of the national flag – red, yellow and green. Here, the airline's sole DC-10 prepares to depart Heathrow for Accra

Below Air Afrique is the international carrier of a consortium of ten African countries, most of which have a strong affiliation with France. The airline has recently added new A300-600Rs to its inventory of A300B4s and A310s, and in turn reduced its DC-10 fleet to a single aircraft. The airline undertakes many weekly flights to Paris/Charles de Gaulle airport, where TU-TAN was photographed in August 1992

Right *Now that all four MD-11s have been delivered, Thai Airways International is actively looking for buyers for its three-strong fleet of DC-10-30s. Wearing the airline's familiar livery is HS-TGE Hariphunchai, inbound to Kai Tak*

Below *Another Asian operator of the DC-10 was Philippine Airlines, who have recently disposed of their two aircraft now that their Boeing 747-400s have been delivered. This photograph of RP-C2114 was taken early in 1987, before the adoption of the present colour scheme*

Below right *Japan Air Lines has been a DC-10 operator since 1976, and along with Northwest is the only user of the series -40. Now that all but two of its MD-11s have been delivered only a handful of the earlier McDonnell-Douglas tri-jets are still in use. Seen in the company's old livery, JA8548 prepares for take-off at Osaka*

Right DC-10-40 JA8538 models JAL's current 'corporate' livery

Below Captured on film during its take-off roll on Kai Tak's runway 13, Japan Air Lines' DC-10-40 JA8542 departs for Tokyo-Narita

Below right In order to enable JAL to operate services to the politically-sensitive Republic of China (Taiwan) without upsetting the People's Republic (mainland China), subsidiary Japan Asia was formed in 1975. The parent company transferred some DC-8s and DC-10s to its affiliate to operate services to Taipei and Kaohsiung, often via Hong Kong. The DC-8s have now been retired and their place taken by a few Boeing 747s, but the DC-10s soldier on. Apart from the tail logo and titling, Japan Asia's close association with JAL is evident in this shot of DC-10-40 JA8531

Above Although a long-established DC-10 operator, Malaysia Airlines has not as yet placed orders for the MD-11. It does, however, operate three MD-11s (one of which is a freighter) on lease from World Airways on regional services alongside newly-delivered Airbus A330s. Seen in Malaysia Airlines' old livery, DC-10-30 9M-MAS was photographed on final approach to Kai Tak

Above left The turquoise Garuda bird stands out well against the dark blue tail of Garuda Indonesia DC-10-30 PK-GIE in this shot taken at Kai Tak. Despite the delivery of six MD-11s, the airline still utilises the same number of DC-10s primarily on regional Asian routes

Left It seems that almost all Asian operators of the DC-10 are on the cusp of disposing them in favour of newer equipment. For example, Bangladesh Biman has advertised its fleet of five aircraft for sale, and has ordered Airbus A310s as replacements. The aircraft featured here, S2-ACP City of Dhaka, was delivered to the airline in 1983, having been one of three acquired from Singapore Airlines

L-1011 TriStar

The Lockheed Aircraft Company is undoubtedly better known for its production of military transport aircraft like the C-130 Hercules and C-5 Galaxy than civil airliners. Indeed, the L-1011 TriStar was the company's first (and to date only) venture into the jet airliner market, and like the DC-10, was primarily conceived due to the American Airlines' requirement for a transcontinental jet. Although American required a twin-jet, other potential customers such as Eastern and Trans World wanted a tri-jet for added safety over long journeys. Lockheed was keen to provide an aircraft with a wider cabin than that offered by the Boeing 707 and Douglas DC-8, which between them dominated the global market.

It soon became obvious to Lockheed that the major threat to the L-1011 came from the proposed Douglas DC-10, which was being developed for the same market, and a tough sales battle was soon in progress. On 29 March 1968 both Eastern and Trans World announced that they had selected the L-1011, named TriStar after Lockheed's tradition of naming its transport aircraft after heavenly bodies. Both orders were for substantial numbers of aircraft, Eastern's order and options totalling 50 aircraft, and TWA requiring 44 – these orders were sufficient for Lockheed to formally launch production, with fabrication being undertaken at Burbank, and final assembly and flight testing at Palmdale. At the latter location a new purpose-built facility was constructed, and like the Boeing 747 plant at Everett, the production facilities were literally built around the prototype aircraft. Assembly began on 24 June 1969, and rather unusually, the fuselage was fully painted prior to mating with the wings. Powered by Rolls-Royce RB211 engines, the prototype took to the sky on 16 November 1970, some two-and-a-half months later than its great rival from Long Beach.

The original version was the L-1011-1, aimed primarily at the US domestic transcontinental market, and of the first 100 aircraft produced all but 21 were series -1 aircraft, many of which went to Delta, Eastern, TWA and Air Canada. By October 1971 Lockheed had received 103 firm orders, and the future was looking rosy indeed. The first order from outside North America was for a modest two aircraft, but these were significant

Below *Delta Airlines has always been the largest operator of the TriStar, and even today the company still flies 56 examples spread over four different variants. llustrated is L-1011-250 N1739D, one of only six TriStar series -250s built. All were operated by Delta, two being built from scratch and four converted from series -1 airframes*

machines as they purchased by Luton-based Court Line, who thus became the world's first charter-operator of 'wide- bodied' jets. These aircraft were delivered early in 1973, and looked resplendent in their eye-catching individual schemes – one was sprayed up in shades of orange, the other pink! Sadly, due to the oil crisis, and the resulting recession in the UK holiday trade, the airline went into liquidation in August 1974, and the aircraft returned to Lockheed – here they sat until being acquired by Cathay Pacific three years later.

Lockheed were no doubt pleased when notable airlines such as All

Nippon and BEA (British European Airways) placed orders for the type, although by now it was becoming apparent that the DC-10 was leading the 'wide-body' tri-jet race. The first of nine TriStar 1s ordered by BEA was delivered to Heathrow in October 1974 in British Airways' livery, as by now BEA and BOAC had amalgamated.

Following on from the series -1, Lockheed produced a further two variants known as the series -100 and -200. They have the same external dimensions as the -1, but offered a significant improvement in range thanks to a slight reduction in their payload capacity. The company also offered the -250, which gave both an improvement in range and an increase in the aircraft's all-up weight. Delta Airlines bought the only two -250s ever built from scratch, and later converted four of its series -1s to this standard. Other conversions from the series -1 include the -50 and -150.

The final TriStar variant was the long range -500, which is instantly recognisable as it has a shorter fuselage length and increased wing span. Lockheed received a boost in August 1976 when British Airways became the launch customer for this ultimate variant, with further orders quickly following for Delta, Pan American and Air Canada. Other customers for

Above and right *Despite their age, TriStars still dominate Delta services to Gatwick. Until recently this London airport was the destination of five daily Delta TriStar flights, interrupted only by the occasional A310. The airline has, however, just announced that the MD-11 is to be introduced on the Atlanta route, signalling perhaps the beginning of the end for Lockheed's tri-jet in Delta's international route network. Captured at the point of rotation, Delta's L-1011-500 N763DL lifts off from Gatwick's runway 26L bound for Cincinnati as flight DL37*

Above *With the undercarriage retracting, L-1011-250 N736DY heads west from Amsterdam's Schiphol airport for another transatlantic crossing. This aircraft was delivered to Delta as a series -1 in March 1982, and converted to its current status in April 1988*

this variant were Air Lanka, Alia - Royal Jordanian, BWIA, LTU, and TAP. Production of the TriStar ended in 1983 with 250 aircraft built – a figure that is considerably less than the production run achieved by the DC-10.

Although not featured in this volume, the TriStar is also in military use with the RAF's No 216 Sqn, nine former BA L-1011-500s having been bought in the 1980s. Seven jets were converted into the tanker/passenger/cargo role and two were retained in passenger-only configuration.

The TriStar has also more recently been involved in the US Space Program, courtesy of Marshall Aerospace of Cambridge. During 1993 the company completed an 18-month long conversion programme to permit a former Air Canada aircraft to carry a large 23-ton Pegasus rocket beneath its belly. The aircraft was delivered to Orbital Sciences Corporation in California on 21 November 1993, and is now used to launch the Pegasus rocket, and its satellite payload, into space, replacing an elderly NASA B-52 previously used in this unique role.

Although many of the major airlines operating TriStars are replacing the type with A330/A340s and Boeing 777s, the L-1011 is finding a new lease of life amongst Third World operators and, in particular, European charter airlines – Swedish carriers Air Ops and Nordic East are leading the way in this area, whilst in the US both American Trans Air and Rich International are avidly increasing their TriStar fleets.

With its 'wide-body' and clean lines, the type also looks like finding a niche for itself as a freighter. Marshalls' have worked closely with Lockheed for many years on C-130s and TriStars, and the company is currently in the process of converting former BA TriStars into freighters for American International Airways, formerly known as Connie Kalitta. Marshalls say there is considerable interest in this programme, and anticipate further orders for such work. A break down of the 250 TriStars built is as follows;

| 123 L-1011-1s, | 19 L-1011-50s, | 21 L-1011-100s, |
| 35 L-1011-200s, | 2 L-1011-250s, | 50 L-1011-500s |

In August 1995 some 199 TriStars were still in service.

Below *Airborne! Launching into the clear blue skies over Gatwick is Delta's N763DL, a series -500 TriStar. Delta currently operates 17 of this variant predominantly on services to Europe – Frankfurt and Gatwick in particular*

Above *A marshaller's eye view of Lockheed's giant tri-jet.as it nears the terminal*

Right *Three Delta TriStars are seen on turn-around at Gatwick's North Terminal*

Right *American Trans Air operates a growing fleet of TriStars, many of which are former Delta aircraft – N192AT is an L-1011-50 which was delivered to Delta as a series -1 in December 1973. During the summer months the opertor's aircraft are frequent visitors on charter flights to European airports, N192AT being seen here during a refuelling stop at Shannon in August 1992*

Below *American Trans Air's is L-1011-50 N192AT. The British Caledonian and Novair tri-jets in this view of the Gatwick ramp date this shot as having been taken in August 1987*

Below right *Rich International is another US charter operator whose TriStar fleet is steadily expanding. Illustrated is L-1011-1 N300AW*

Left *Trans World Airlines (TWA) is a long-established TriStar operator that has struggled on over the past decade despite severe financial problems. In recent years the airline has slowly been disposing of its large tri-jets, and at the time of writing only 15 TriStars remain in use. Illustrated on approach to Athens is L-1011-50 N31018, this aircraft having been delivered to TWA in March 1974, but sold to Air Ops of Europe early in 1995*

Below left *Hawaiian Airlines N765BE (L-1011-50) shows off its stylish livery against the backdrop of snow-capped mountains at Seattle. Hawaiian acquired TriStars for use on its transpacific routes from Honolulu, although the type has recently been replaced by former American Airlines DC-10s. This aircraft was originally delivered to All Nippon, and has now been sold on to Rich International*

Below *Immaculate Eastern Airlines Tristar 1 N333EA turns onto the runway at Miami. Following the demise of its once huge owners, this aircraft was briefly stored at Mojave, but like several other former Eastern aircraft it was acquired by Delta and put to work on the latter's domestic routes*

Above Air Canada was an early customer for the TriStar, initially operating series -1 machines within North America which were later joined by long-range -500s for European routes. Seen lining up for departure from runway 27L at Heathrow is -500 C-GAGK. This particular aircraft now serves with Delta as N769DL

Left Struggling to keep costs down in the recession-struck 1990s, Air Canada decided to dispose of its fleet of TriStars and concentrate on the Boeing 747 and 767 for long-range services. However, during the early part of 1994 the airline realised it was facing a shortage of capacity for the forthcoming summer, and in a surprise move regenerated three TriStars from desert storage for use within North America, and particularly the Los Angeles route. One of these aircraft was -1 C-FTND, which is seen at Toronto resplendent in the airline's new livery

Above *TriStar C-FTNA was an early build -1 which, although delivered to Eastern Airlines in December 1972 as N312EA, spent much of the next ten years on lease to Air Canada. It has since been converted to -150 standard and is now operated by Canadian charter airline Air Transat. During the summer months its aircraft are heavily utilised on charter flights to Europe*

Above right *Due to its high capacity and long range, the TriStar has proven popular for short term leases. During 1994 Tunisair leased Air Atlanta Iceland's L-1011-100 TF-ABM*

Right *Royal Aviation is a Canadian charter airline which was founded in 1991, initially with Boeing 727 equipment. For the 1994 summer season it acquired two TriStar 100s which were heavily utilised on services to Glasgow, Manchester and London/Gatwick. Illustrated at the latter location is C-FTNI, a former Air Canada machine*

Above *Showing the TriStar's clean lines in the current Royal Jordanian Airlines livery is L-1011-500 JY-AGA*

Right *At first glance this TriStar 500 is simply a Royal Jordanian Airlines machine. However, despite wearing the carrier's impressive livery, the titling, 'The Hashemite Kingdom of Jordan' identifies it as the personal transport of King Hussein – note the appropriate registration JY-HKJ*

Right *Saudia took delivery of its first TriStar in June 1975, and currently operates 17 series -200s. Of the seven TriStars which have been written off in accidents, the crash of Saudia's HZ-AHK at Riyadh on 19 August 1980 incurred the highest loss of life with all 301 passengers and crew aboard being killed. Saudia's TriStars are utilised on most of the company's European routes, including Geneva where HZ-AHR was photographed at the point of rotation*

Below right *Gulf Air acquired TriStar 200s to replace its VC10s on international routes. These aircraft have now in turn been replaced by a sizeable fleet of Boeing 767s and Airbus A340s, with a number of the now-redundent L-1011s being earmarked for conversion to freighters by Marshall Aerospace. Photographed about to depart from Heathrow is aircraft A40-TY*

Below *One of the latest airlines to add the TriStar to its inventory is Hong Kong's Dragonair. Two series -1 aircraft were acquired on lease from Cathay Pacific in 1993 primarily for use on routes to Beijing and Shanghai. However, by the autumn of 1995 the type had served its purpose, and both jets were disposed of in order to make way for three new Airbus A330s. L-1011-1 VR-HMW was photographed about to depart Kai Tak for Shanghai in November 1994*

Right Swedish charter airline Nordic East has recently joined the TriStar club with the acquisition in 1995 of two former Cathay Pacific L-1011-1s. This aircraft, SE-DTD, was formerly VR-HMV with Cathay, and prior to its spell in Hong Kong had served with both LTU and Eastern Airlines

Left Although Air Ops of Europe is also a Swedish-owned charter airline that utilises the TriStar, so many of its aircraft operate inclusive tour flights from Gatwick and Manchester that you would think they were a British company. The origin of TriStar 50 SE-DPP is blatantly obvious as the aircraft is predominantly still in its former Hawaiian Air livery. Note the additional ECU Air titles and the name Olivia on the nose

Below *Another view of Air Ops SE-DPP in its Hawaiian colours, but this time with the addition of Sudan Airways titling. The aircraft was contracted to operate a weekly Gatwick - Khartoum - Johannesburg service for the African carrier until replaced by a Skyjet DC-10*

Right *During 1995 Air Ops' TriStar fleet has increased to eight aircraft and, after a period where the fleet sported a number of varied colour schemes belonging to previous operators, the company eventually standardised on its own livery. Former TWA TriStar 1, SE-DPV sports the newly-adopted colours.*

Left *Air Atlanta Iceland has recently expanded its fleet with the acquisition of several elderly Boeing 747s and two Lockheed L-1011 TriStars to supplement its Boeing 737s. During the 1995 European summer holiday season the airline's aircraft were particularly active, operating a number of sub charters on behalf of several major charter firms. Photographed at the end of July 1995, L-1011-1 TF-ABL was operating on behalf of Monarch at the time. The green cheatline is a legacy of its previous spell with Cathay Pacific*

Below *British Airways has sold its shareholding in Caledonian, a move which will see the charter airline's Boeing 757s and one of its DC-10s returned to the state airline. Displaying Caledonian's pleasing livery to good effect is L-1011 TriStar 100 G-BBAF Loch Fyne*

Right *Gatwick-based Caledonian Airways is now the sole British operator of the TriStar. The airline currently uses five former British Airways aircraft on charter flights throughout Europe. Illustrated at its base is L-1011-100 G-BBAE Loch Earn*

Above The golden lion stands proud as TriStar 100 G-BBAH Loch Avon climbs into the winter skies over Gatwick, bound for the warmer climate of Tenerife

Left L-1011-100 G-BBAE Loch Earn defies gravity and climbs away from Gatwick's runway. This photograph was taken in 1992, hence the Dan-Air aircraft in the background

Below *Now that its Airbus A340s have been delivered, Air Portugal is in the process of disposing of its five TriStar 500s which entered service in 1983. Photographed a long way from home at Rio de Janeiro's Galeao International airport is CS-TED*

Right *British Airways disposed of its TriStars when sufficient numbers of Boeing 767s were delivered. Shining like a new pin is L-1011-100 G-BBAH* Lyme Bay. *This aircraft was delivered in January 1975 and was initially named* The Sunsilk Rose, *but now plies its trade in Caledonian colours*

Right Another airline disposing of its TriStars is German charter company LTU - Lufttransport-Unternehmen. The Dusseldorf-based airline has recently completed a modernisation programme that has seen it acquire four MD-11s and five A330s. Taxying clear of the runway is long range L-1011-500 D-AERT, an aircraft which has spent its entire operational life with LTU since its delivery from Lockheed in April 1980

Below Dragonair's TriStar 1 VR-HMW is seen about to land at Kai Tak

Right *Cathay Pacific Airlines began operating the TriStar with the acquisition of two series -100s in 1975. Over the years a considerable number of series -1s were added to the inventory, including a number of former Eastern Airlines machines in the late 1980s – L-1011-1 VR-HOC is one such aircraft, being acquired from Eastern in 1987*

Left *Cathay's TriStars have been regular visitors to most major Asian airports over the past two decades. About to touch down at Nagoya, in Japan, is L-1011-1 VR-HHY. Now that Airbus A330s and A340s are being delivered, the airline is rapidly disposing of its TriStar fleet*

Left VR-HHL is one of a pair of series -100 TriStars which served with Cathay. This photograph was taken at, or to be more precise, over Kai Tak in 1987, when the airline's tri-jets were emblazoned with 'Super TriStar' titling on the fin.

Below With the numerous tower blocks in the background this shot could only have been taken in Hong Kong. Taxying away from a typically crowded ramp is Cathay L-1011-1 VR-HOI, formerly Eastern's N318EA. This photograph was taken in November 1994, and it is noticeable that with the impending Chinese takeover of Hong Kong approaching in 1997, the airline has dispensed with the Union Jack on the fin of their aircraft

Above left *All Nippon Airways acquired a substantial number of TriStars for use on its high-density domestic routes, as at the time of their purchase it was purely a domestic airline not permitted to compete with flag carrier Japan Air Lines. All Nippon ultimately operated four variants of Lockheed's tri-jet, namely the -1, -50, -100 and -200, and the airline is currently in the throes of disposing of the last of the type. Illustrated about to depart Osaka is L-1011-1 JA8519*

Left *Another Asian carrier disposing the last of its TriStars is Air Lanka, who operated four TriStar variants – the -50, -100, -200 and -500, all of which have been replaced by Airbus A340s. Turning onto Heathrow's runway 27L ready for take-off is TriStar 500 4R-ULC* City of Anuradhapura

Above *TriStars of BWIA (British West Indian A\rlines) International have been regular visitors to London Heathrow for many years. The company operates four long range L-1011-500s, the first of which was delivered in January 1980. BWIA has recently announced that it is to modernise its fleet, with Boeing 767s slated to replace the tri-jets in the not too distant future. TriStar 500 9Y-TGN is seen here seconds away from landing at London's premier airport on a winter's morning*

MD-11

To succeed the popular DC-10 McDonnell Douglas came up with the MD-11, details of which were first released at the 1985 Paris Airshow. The following year the company gave the go-ahead for the MD-11, even though the DC-10 was still in production at the time. Assembly of the first aircraft began in March 1988, with the first flight scheduled for the following summer – shortly after DC-10 production was due to cease.

At first glance it could be said that the MD-11 is just a DC-10 with a longer fuselage and winglets, but nothing could be further from the truth. The use of composite materials such as carbon-fibre, glass-fibre and Kevlar in over 20 of the airframe components have reduced the aircraft's all up weight significantly, whilst the winglets, and additional aerodynamic improvements, offer a much increased performance over the DC-10.

McDonnell Douglas salesmen were quickly knocking on the doors of prospective customers, enthusing over the MD-11s advertised 27 per cent improvement in range and 31 per cent reduction in seat/mile costs when compared to the DC-10-30. Additional cost savings were made by the use of improved avionics and glass-cockpit technology, thereby dispensing with the flight engineer and reducing the flightdeck crew to two pilots.

No doubt McDonnell Douglas were hoping that many existing DC-10 customers would choose the MD-11 as a successor, and from the outset the company offered three variants. The straight passenger variant can seat from 234 in a mixed configuration up to a maximum of 410 in an all-economy fit. The capacity and range offered in this fit makes the MD-11 an attractive proposition for charter carriers, and Germany's LTU operates its MD-11s in an all-economy 408 seat configuration.

Left *Delta Airlines was the second customer to take delivery of McDonnell Douglas's new tri-jet, its first aircraft arriving one month after Finnair had received its first MD-11. The airline has recently introduced the type on services to Frankfurt, but they are predominantly used on transpacific routes. Illustrated taxying for departure at Hong Kong's Kai Tak airport is MD-11 N804DE, this aircraft having been delivered to the airline in May 1992*

Following on the success of the DC-10-30CF, the company also offers customers a Combi variant with a side-loading cargo door in the rear fuselage. The all-freighter MD-11F features a forward fuselage side cargo door, and is devoid of windows. This version can carry 26 cargo pallets on the main deck with additional space for smaller containers in the belly hold. This was the choice of launch customer Federal Express.

McDonnell Douglas has since come up with the Convertible Freighter variant which differs from the Combi in that in can be used either in the all-passenger or all-freighter roles, and therefore features the forward side cargo door as on the MD-11F. The variant is ideal for customers who, like Martinair of Holland, have seasonal markets whereby the aircraft can be used for passenger work in summer and as a freighter in winter. The company is now also offering an ER (extended range) variant, made possible by reducing the fuselage drag and increasing fuel capacity.

The MD-11's maiden voyage at the hands of British test pilot John Miller took place on 10 January 1990, more than six months later than originally planned. This aircraft, N111MD, is an MD-11F(AF) freighter and, like the second prototype, was used in the flight test and certification programme before being handed over to FedEx in the summer of 1991.

The initial launch customer for the MD-11 was British Caledonian who, on 3 December 1986, placed an order for three with options on a further six. Unfortunately for McDonnell Douglas British Caledonian was soon taken over by British Airways, who promptly cancelled the order. This is despite the fact that BA required a replacement for its TriStars, and was favourably impressed by the performance of the eight DC-10s it

Above During a visit to Portland, Oregon, in February 1993 the author was amazed when in the space of an hour no less than five Delta MD-11s landed – the airline uses this north-west airport as a hub for its transpacific MD-11 operations. Seen climbing out of Portland, bound for Tokyo, as flight DL51 is MD-11 N807DE. This aircraft had only been delivered to the airline two months earlier

Left Although American Airlines has not openly criticised the performance of the MD-11, it must be assumed that the carrier is not altogether satisfied with it as during the period 1996-99, 12 aircraft are to be sold off to FedEx for conversion into freighters. The remaining seven aircraft are likely to follow at a later date. Seen here on a crisp winters day, MD-11 N1763 was photographed on short finals to Heathrow

Overleaf American Airlines attaches the title 'Luxury Liner' to its fleet of MD-11s. A highly-polished example of the type awaits departure clearance from Gatwick, bound for Dallas/Fort Worth

inherited from British Caledonian. Those DC-10s are still in daily use by the airline, and there are no immediate plans to replace them despite the delivery of their first Boeing 777s – indeed one of the two currently leased to Caledonian Airways is being recalled to the BA inventory as it is required by the airline for its 1996 operations.

Another potential British MD-11 operator was Air Europe who ordered six with 12 options, all to be powered by Rolls-Royce RB211 engines. Unfortunately this emerging airline was forced to cease operations due to the financial problems of its parent company.

The first aircraft to enter customer service was the ninth aircraft built, and was delivered to Finnair in November 1990. This was followed by two deliveries to Delta Airlines the following month. The largest customer to date is American Airlines who have 19 aircraft, the first of which was delivered February 1991. By February 1990 the prospects for the MD-11 were looking very good indeed, with orders and options totalling 340 – only 106 short of the total DC-10 production. The MD-11 was already leaping ahead of its prospective main rivals, the Airbus A330/A340 and the Boeing 777. Soon afterwards, however, it became apparent that the MD-11 was not meeting its advertised range/payload specifications, and customer dissatisfaction with the new jet was making the headlines in the aviation press.

Much of the criticism of the type's performance, or lack of, stemmed from Asian airlines, with whom it had initially sold in fairly well. There is no doubt the adverse criticism has affected sales, as many customers cancelled orders and options, to the effect that by June 1994 total commitments to the type had shrunk to just 264 airframes. The manufacturer has in the meantime been working hard to improve the performance, specifically reducing the drag. It carried out enhancements to jets already delivered at no extra cost, but there is no doubt that confidence in the MD-11 has been affected, and by August 1995 only 137 were in use with 20 customers, and just 27 orders were outstanding.

Although the airline has not openly criticised the type, Korean Air has already commenced converting its five virtually new aircraft into freighters. Similarly, American Airlines, for whom the type is the largest in its inventory, is to sell its MD-11s to Fedex, who will in turn convert them to freighter configuration.

Right US charter operator World Airways has replaced its entire fleet of DC-10s with McDonnell Douglas's newest tri-jet. The airline currently has five aircraft in use, with a further two on order. These comprise both passenger and freighter variants, and one of each is currently on lease to Malaysia Airlines. The passenger variant leased to the Asian airline is N273WA, which is seen here in full World livery

Below Brazil's Varig has operated the DC-10 for many years, and the MD-11 was seen as a natural successor. Varig currently has six MD-11s in service, all of which are leased. Despite this, the DC-10s still soldier on, no doubt due to the airline's decision to dispose of almost all its leased 747s in an effort to reduce costs. The company's MD-11s are now used on all its European routes, including to Zurich, where PP-VOQ was photographed

Right FedEx has used the DC-10-30F for a number of years, and now has 13 MD-11 freighters in use, with a further four on order. It is also due to take most, if not all, of American Airlines MD-11s. The adoption of the new company name was seen as the perfect opportunity to introduce a revised livery, as featured on MD-11F(AF) N601FE seen on approach to Kai Tak

The MD-11 is certainly finding a niche for itself in the long-range freight market, but further development, and its future as a long-range passenger airliner, may well depend on customers being confident that it can meet its performance specifications. If it can do so, then it will have proved itself a worthy successor to the DC-10.

Turning to designations, the company has used the F suffix for any MD-11 which has a cargo door, hence the Combi variant has the designation MD-11F(C).

Below Another Brazilian MD-11 operator is Sao Paulo-based VASP, the airline currently operating four of the type. It has also recently signed a leasing agreement for a further two jets, and is also expected to take one of KLM's aircraft on lease. MD-11 PP-SOZ was photographed at Rio de Janeiro's Galeao International Airport sporting the airline's attractive blue livery

Inset The largest non-US operator of the MD-11 is Swissair, an airline which had previously operated the DC-10 for many years. The Swiss national carrier took delivery of its first MD-11 in March 1991, and now has 13 in use, with one more on order. A single aircraft is flown in Swissair Asia titles, allowing the airline to serve Taipei without incurring the wrath of Beijing! Lining-up on runway 13 at Kai Tak is MD-11 HB-IWL

Below The MD-11 has made inroads into the European inclusive tour charter market with the delivery of four aircraft to Germany's LTU, where they have replaced the TriStar. The type is heavily utilised on flights to the Canary Islands, particularly Las Palmas, where D-AERZ (the airline's fourth MD-11) was photographed

Right Alitalia is another former DC-10 operator, although the Italian flag carrier disposed of its DC-10s long before the first of its eight MD-11s was delivered in November 1991. Alitalia operates a mixture of passenger and combi variants, one of the latter being MD-11F(C) I-DUPU Ponte Vecchio, which was photographed turning onto final approach for runway 13 at Kai Tak

Above *The fuselage-mounted centre-line bogie is clearly visible in this shot of Alitalia MD-11 I-DUPC* Vincente Bellini

Right *Due to the mountainous terrain, and associated wind currents, the approach to runway 13 at Kai Tak is without a doubt one of the most demanding and potentially hazardous to be encountered anywhere in the world. These days pilots seldom get it wrong — however, when they do, it usually brings a string of exclamations from those who witness the event. In this instance the pilot of Alitalia MD-11 I-DUPB is way below the nominal glidepath, and is literally skimming the rooftops. Indeed, this aircraft was so low it disappeared from view behind the tree at the right hand edge of the picture. Thankfully, the aircraft landed safely, albeit it in the 'sterile' portion of runway 13 reserved for take-offs only!*

Left Dutch airline Martinair has disposed of its fleet of DC-10s, two of which have been purchased by the Royal Netherlands Air Force and converted into tanker/cargo aircraft. As replacements, four MD-11F(CF) aircraft were delivered during 1995, with a further aircraft on order. These jets are used on charter flights on high-density European holiday routes, as well as on long-range services. Seen on push-back at Amsterdam/Schiphol is PH-MCR, the second MD-11 delivered to the airline

Above KLM - Royal Dutch Airlines is in the process of taking delivery of a fleet of 10 MD-11s, three of which had yet to arrive when this book went to press. The Dutch airline is another which has replaced its DC-10s with the MD-11, although it has also recently taken delivery of its first Boeing 767, and rumours abound that it is to dispose of its new tri-jets, possibly to Northwest, in favour of more 767s. MD-11 PH-KCE Audrey Hepburn is seen having just got airborne from Amsterdam Schiphol's runway 24

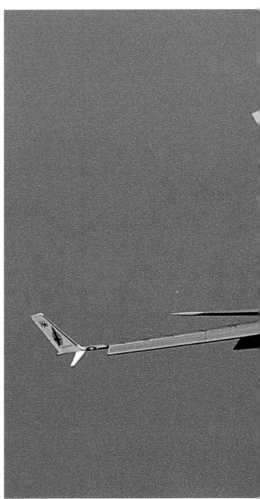

Left *Illustrated at Las Palmas is Finnair's OH-LGA, this aircraft having made history on 29 November 1990 when it became the first MD-11 to be delivered to a customer. By Christmas the aircraft had entered service with Finnair on its transpolar route to Tokyo, replacing the DC-10. The airline also utilises the type on high-density charter routes to destinations such as Las Palmas*

Below left *Japan Air Lines is replacing its DC-10s with 10 MD-11s, eight of which have been delivered to date. The airline has taken the opportunity to personalise its fleet of new tri-jets by naming each aircraft after a bird, an illustration of which appears on the winglets and fuselage. Aircraft JA8581 was the airline's second MD-11 to be delivered, and is named* Fairy Pitta

Below *Inbound to Hong Kong is JAL's first MD-11 'J-Bird' JA8580*

Left *Shanghai-based China Eastern Airlines was an early MD-11 customer from the Far East, operating six jets, one of which is a freighter. The passenger variants are regular visitors to Hong Kong, where B-2173 was photographed about to land*

Above *The MD-11 has proved a popular choice of Asian airlines, and for aficionados of the type Hong Kong is the place to be, as no less than 12 MD-11 operators serve Kai Tak airport. Taxying onto the runway for the short flight to Taipei is B-153 of China Airlines*

Below *Thai Airways International has received four MD-11s to replace its three DC-10s, which are now up for sale. One of its MD-11s, HS-TMD, was substantially damaged at Bangkok on 22 October 1994 when it jumped its wheel chocks and rammed a parked A300 during engine runs. As yet the aircraft has still not been repaired, and remains grounded at the airlines' Thai base. Sister aircraft HS-TMF was photographed on its take-off run at Kai Tak*

Right *China Airlines has taken delivery of four MD-11s, although two of these, including aircraft B-150, are currently operated by subsidiary Mandarin Airlines*

Top Korean Airlines is another Asian operator which would appear to be less than satisfied with the performance of its fleet of five MD-11s. An early customer for the jet, with the first of the type being delivered in February 1991, Korean is converting all five of its aircraft into pure freighters – the first airframe was completed in mid-1995. The remaining four MD-11s were to have been converted in South Korea, but this work is now to be undertaken in the US. Wearing 'World Cup 2002' stickers, HL7371 begins its take-off roll from Amsterdam/Schiphol

Above Although it has taken delivery of six MD-11s, Garuda Indonesia seems in no hurry to dispose of its fleet of DC-10s. The airline received its first MD-11, leased from Guiness-Peat, in December 1991, but relations between the airline, the lessor and manufacturer have been somewhat less than harmonious, with Garuda claiming that the aircraft's inability to meet performance specifications has cost it large sums of money in lost revenue. Indeed, the airline has already stated that when sufficient Boeing 747 400s have been delivered the MD-11s will be returned to the lessor

Specifications and Users

DC-10

DC-10-10

First flight date	29 August 1970
Wing span	47.35 m (155 ft 4 in)
Length	55.3 m (181 ft 5 in)
Height	17.7 m 58 ft 1 in
Max accommodation	380
Max take-off weight	185,970kg (410,000 lb)
Max cruising speed	928 km/h (501 kt, 577 mph)
Max range	4355 km (2350 nm)

DC-10-15

First flight date	8 January 1981
Wing span	47.35 m (155 ft 4 in)
Length	55.5 m (182 ft 1 in)
Height	17.7 m (58 ft 1 in)
Max accommodation	380
Max take-off weight	206,385 kg (455,000 lb)
Max cruising speed	928 km/h (501 kt, 577 mph)
Max range	6850 km (3700 nm)

DC-10-30

First flight date	21 June 1972
Wing span	50.4 m (165 ft 4 in)
Length	55.5 m (182 ft 1 in)
Height	17.7 m (58 ft 1 in)
Max accommodation	380
Max take-off weight	263,085 kg (580,000 lb)
Max cruising speed	908km/h (490kt, 564 mph)
Max range	7413 km (4000 nm)

DC-10-40

First flight date	28 February 1972
Wing span	50.4 m (165 ft 4 in)
Length	55.5 m (182 ft 1 in)
Height	17.7 m (58 ft 1 in)
Max accommodation	380
Max take-off weight	259,459 kg (572,000 lb)
Max cruising speed	922 km/h (498 kt, 573 mph)
Max range	7505 km (4050 nm)

L-1011 TriStar

L-1011-1

First flight date	16 November 1970
Wing span	47.34 m (155 ft 4 in)
Length	54.17 m (177 ft 8 in)
Height	16.87 m (55 ft 4 in)
Max accommodation	400
Max take-off weight	195,045 kg (430,000 lb)
Max cruising speed	964 km/h (520 kt, 599 mph)
Max range	5319 km (2870 nm)

L-1011-100

First flight date	25 April 1975
Wing span	47.34 m (155 ft 4 in)
Length	54.17 m (177 ft 8 in)
Height	16.87 m (55 ft 4 in)
Max accommodation	400
Max take-off weight	211,375 kg (466,000 lb)
Max cruising speed	954 km/h (515 kt, 593 mph)
Max range	6783 km (3660 nm)

L-1011-200

First flight date	8 October 1976
Wing span	47.34 m (155 ft 4 in)
Length	54.17 m (177 ft 8 in)
Height	16.87 m (55 ft 4 in)
Max accommodation	400
Max take-off weight	211,375 kg (466,000 lb)
Max cruising speed	982 km/h (530 kt, 610 mph)
Max range	6820 km (3680 nm)

L-1011-250

First flight date	December 1986
Wing span	47.34 m (155 ft 4 in)
Length	54.17 m (177 ft 8 in)
Height	16.87 m (55 ft 4 in)
Max accommodation	400
Max take-off weight	231,438 kg (510,000 lb)
Max cruising speed	973 km/h (525 kt, 605 mph)
Max range	8376 km (4520 nm)

L-1011-500

First flight date	16 October 1978
Wing span	50.06 m (164 ft 4 in)
Length	50.05 m (164 ft 2 in)
Height	16.87 m (55 ft 4 in)
Max accommodation	330
Max take-off weight	224,980 kg (496,000 lb)
Max cruising speed	973 km/h (525 kt, 605 mph)
Max range	9748 km (5260 nm)

MD-11

MD-11(Basic)

First flight date	26 April 1990
Wing span	51.8 m (169 ft 8 in)
Length	61.4 m (201 ft 3 in)
Height	17.6 m (57 ft 9 in)
Max accommodation	410
Max take-off weight	283,722 kg (625,500 lb)
Max cruising speed	945 km/h (511 kt, 588 mph)
Max range	12,569 km (6787 nm)

MD-11F(C)

First flight date	October 1991
Wing span	51.8 m (169 ft 8 in)
Length	61.4 m (201 ft 3 in)
Height	17.6 m (57 ft 9 in)
Max accommodation	410
Max take-off weight	283,722 kg (625,500 lb)
Max cruising speed	945 km/h (511 kt, 588 mph)
Max range	11,611 km (6269 nm)

MD-11F(AF)

First flight date	10 January 1990
Wing span	51.8 m (169 ft 8 in)
Length	61.4 m (201 ft 3 in)
Height	17.6 m (57 ft 9 in)
Max accommodation	Nil
Max take-off weight	283,722 kg (625,500 lb)
Max cruising speed	945 km/h (511 kt, 588 mph)
Max range	6711 km (3623 nm)

MD-11F(CF)

First flight date	November 1994
Wing span	51.8 m (169 ft 8 in)
Length	61.4 m (201 ft 3 in)
Height	17.6 m (57 ft 9 in)
Max accommodation	410
Max take-off weight	285,990 kg (630,500 lb)
Max cruising speed	945 km/h (511 kt, 588 mph)
Max range	12,468 km (6735 nm)

Current operators and fleet size (as at 1 October 1995)

DC-10

Aeroflot – Russian International Airlines 2
Aeromexico 3
Aeroperu 2
African Safari I
Air Afrique I
Air Liberte 3
Aom – French Airlines 13
American Airlines 22
Arca Colombia I
Bangladesh Biman Airlines 5
British Airways 6
Caledonian Airways 2
Canadian Airlines International 10
Challengair I
Condor Flugdienst 5
Continental Airlines 14
Continental Micronesia 5
Corsair I
FedEx 35
Finnair I
Garuda Indonesia 6
Ghana Airways I
Hawaiian Air 6
Iberia 7
Japan Air Lines 13
Japan Air Charter 3
Japan Air System 2
Japan Asia Airways 4
Korean Air 3
Kras Air 2
LOT I
Malaysia Airlines 4
Mexicana I
Nigeria Airways 2
Northwest Airlines 29
Pluna 2
Premiair 4
Project Orbis I
Royal Netherlands Air Force (KDC-10) 2
Sabena 2
Skyjet I
Skyjet Brazil I
Sun Country Airlines 6
Tarom I
Thai Airways International 3
United Airlines 38
United States Air Force (KC-10A) 59
Varig 9
VASP I
Viasa 5
World Airways 3

* On Order

L-1011

Air Atlanta Iceland 2
Air Canada 3
Air Lanka. 4
Air Ops Europe 8
Air Portugal 4
Air Transat 5
All Nippon Airways 3
American International Airways 4
American Trans Air 14
Apa Internacional I
British West Indian Airlines (BWIA) 5
Caledonian Airways 5
Cathay Pacific 9
Delta Airlines 56
Faucett/Aero Peru I
Istanbul Airlines I
Jordanian Royal Flight I
LTU 5
Nordic East Airways 2
Orbital Sciences Corporation I
Pat Robertson Operation Blessing I
Rich International 11
Royal Air Force 9
Royal Jordanian Airlines 5
Saudia 17
Saudi Royal Flight/Government 2
TAAG Angola I
Tajikistan International Airlines 2
Trans World Airlines 15

MD-11

Alitalia 8
American Airlines 19
China Airlines 2
China Eastern Airlines 6
Delta Airlines . . . . 11 + 4*
Eva Air 6
FedEx . . . . 13 + 4*
Finnair 4
Garuda Indonesia . . . . 6 + 3*
Ghana Airways I
Japan Air Lines . . . . 8 + 2*
KLM . . . . 7 + 3*
Korean Air 5
LTU 4
Mandarin Airlines 2
Malaysia Airlines 3
Martinair . . . . 4 + 1*
Polynesian Airlines I
Swissair 13
Swissair Asia I
Thai Airways International 4
Varig 6
VASP . . . . 4 + 2*
World Airways . . . . 5 + 2*